cyc
11/08

Blizzards

by Lisa Bullard

PULL AHEAD BOOKS
Forces of Nature

Lerner Publications Company • Minneapolis

For my brother Dan, with love, for sharing all of those snow days with me

Photo Acknowledgments

The images in this book are used with the permission of: © Photodisc/Getty Images, p. 1, all backgrounds; © Robert Giroux/Getty Images, p. 4; © Christopher Pillitz/Reportage/Getty Images, p. 6; © David Jay Zimmerman/CORBIS, p. 7; © John Beatty/Photo Researchers, Inc., p. 8; AP Photo/Peter M. Fredin, p. 9; © Reuters/CORBIS, pp. 10, 12; AP Photo/Charlie Neibergall, p. 11; © Benjamin Lowy/CORBIS, p. 14; AP Photo/Wyoming Highway Patrol, p. 15; © Ralph Orlowski/Getty Images, p. 16; © China Photos/Getty Images, p. 18; © SIU/Visuals Unlimited, p. 19; © Scientifica/Visuals Unlimited, p. 20; © KEN HAWKINS/CORBIS SYGMA, p. 22; AP Photo/The Patriot-News, Amiran White, p. 24; © Stockbyte/Getty Images, p. 26; © Jochen Sand/Riser/Getty Images, p. 27; © Bill Hauser/Independent Picture Service, p. 28. Front Cover: AP Photo/Benny Snyder.

Lerner Publications Company
A division of Lerner Publishing Group, Inc.
241 First Avenue North
Minneapolis, MN 55401 U.S.A.

Website address: www.lernerbooks.com

Words in **bold type** are explained in a glossary on page 31.

Library of Congress Cataloging-in-Publication Data

Bullard, Lisa.
    Blizzards / by Lisa Bullard.
       p.   cm. — (Pull ahead books. Forces of nature)
    Includes index.
    ISBN-13: 978-0-8225-8828-3 (lib. bdg. : alk. paper)
    1. Blizzards—Juvenile literature. I. Title
QC926.37.B835 2009
551.55'5—dc22   2007030535

Manufactured in the United States of America
1 2 3 4 5 6 – BP – 14 13 12 11 10 09

Table of Contents

What Is a Blizzard?

Cold winds blast. Cars are buried under snowdrifts. Why has the world turned white?

This monster storm is called a **blizzard**.

Blizzards are storms with blowing snow and cold. But not all snowstorms are blizzards.

It takes a strong wind to turn a
snowstorm into a blizzard.

A scientist uses a special tool to measure wind speed.

Blizzard winds blow 35 miles (56 kilometers) per hour or more. They last for at least three hours.

The strong winds swirl any falling snow.
Winds pick up more snow from the
ground.

Blowing snow in the air makes it very hard to see. People can become lost while walking or driving.

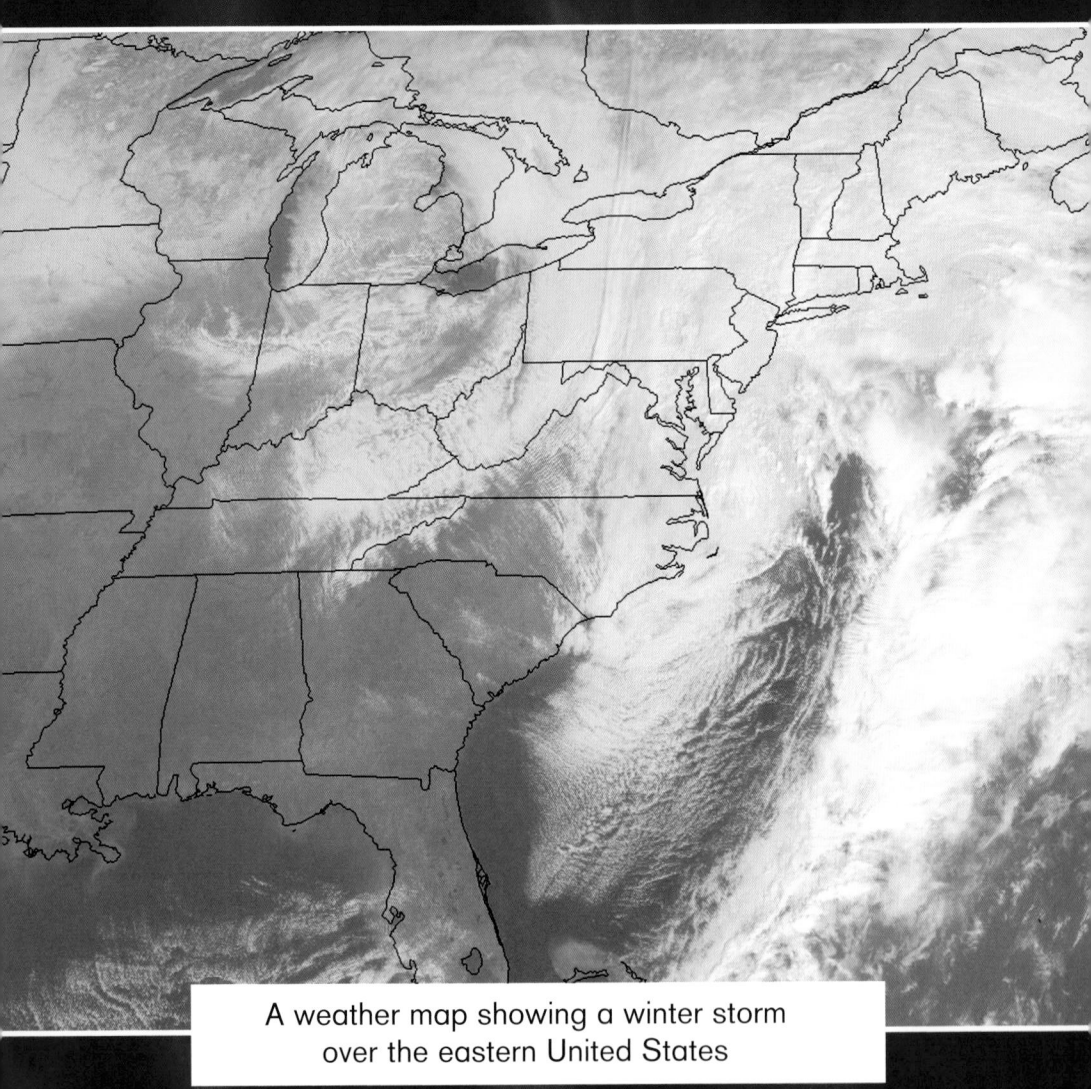

A weather map showing a winter storm
over the eastern United States

Where Blizzards Happen

Blizzards happen most often in the countries of Canada, Russia, and the United States. Most blizzards in the United States happen in the north central and northeastern states.

Most snowstorms do not become blizzards. There might be only a few blizzards in the United States each year.

New York City during a blizzard in 2003

But these storms can kill people.

Heavy snow made this roof cave in.

Dangers of Blizzards

Snow and ice make roads very slippery. Some people die in car accidents. Roofs can cave in from the heavy snow and crush people. People can die of heart attacks while shoveling. During a blizzard, the **temperature** can become very cold.

Strong winds make it feel even colder. This is known as **windchill**. People and animals should not stay outside too long in this weather. They can freeze to death.

If you have to go outside during a blizzard, you should cover as much of your skin as possible.

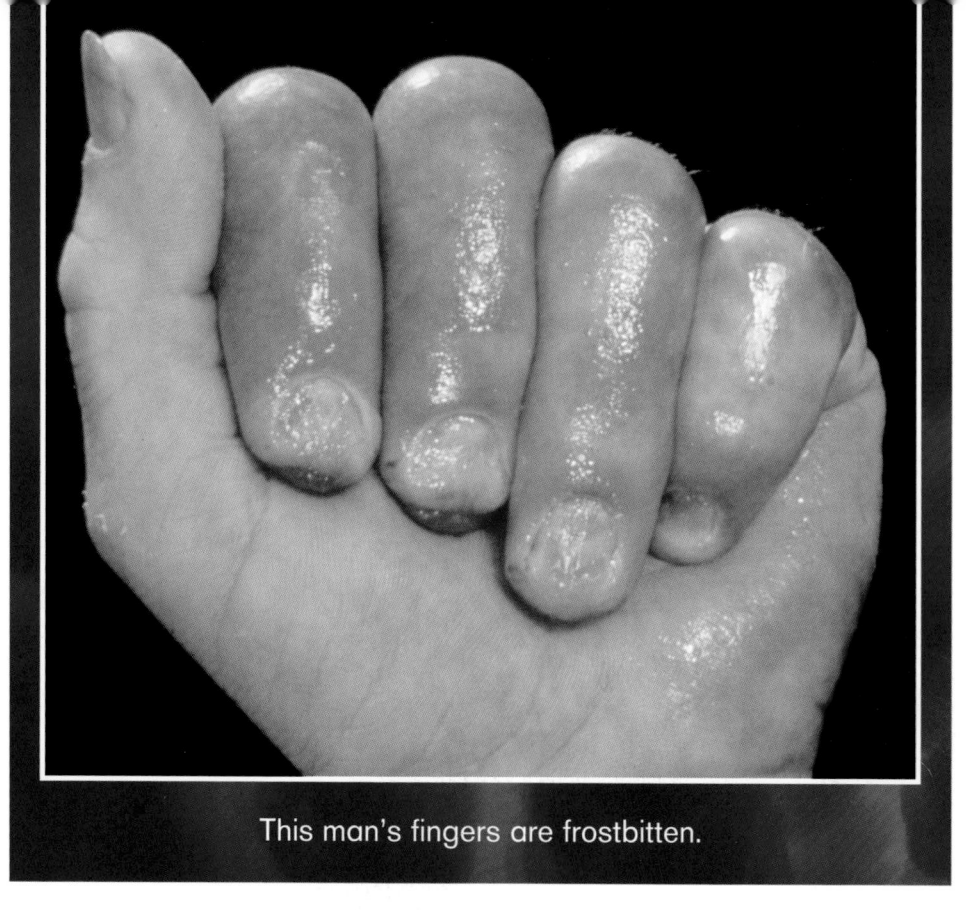
This man's fingers are frostbitten.

People can get **frostbite**. The cold
freezes a part of their bodies. Frostbite
often happens to fingers, toes, or ears.

A **meteorologist** uses computers
to track storms.

Tracking Blizzards

Scientists who study the weather are called meteorologists. They try to warn everyone before blizzards strike. They use computers and other tools to track storms. But they cannot always tell when or where a blizzard will hit. Blizzards often take people by surprise.

This girl in Atlanta, Georgia, slides in the snow
left behind by the Storm of the Century.

Storm of the Century

A huge blizzard in 1993 surprised many people. It was called the Storm of the Century. The blizzard hit 26 states. Heavy snow fell in states that rarely get snow. Winds blew over 100 miles (161 km) per hour at times. More than four feet (1.2 meters) of snow fell in some places. The storm even caused several **tornadoes**. More than 270 people died.

A **snowmobile** drives on a street covered
with snow in Harrisburg, Pennsylvania.

Staying Safe

People who live in cold places watch for blizzard warnings. They stay home. They wear many layers of clothing to stay warm. They try not to drive on slippery streets. Some people have snowmobiles. They can still get around when roads are covered with snow.

Snow is an important source of Earth's water. But the wildest snowstorms are also dangerous.

Don't take chances in a blizzard. Wait inside until it is safe to go out and play!

BLIZZARD WEATHER

Blizzards can form when a warm, moist weather system meets a cold, dry weather system.

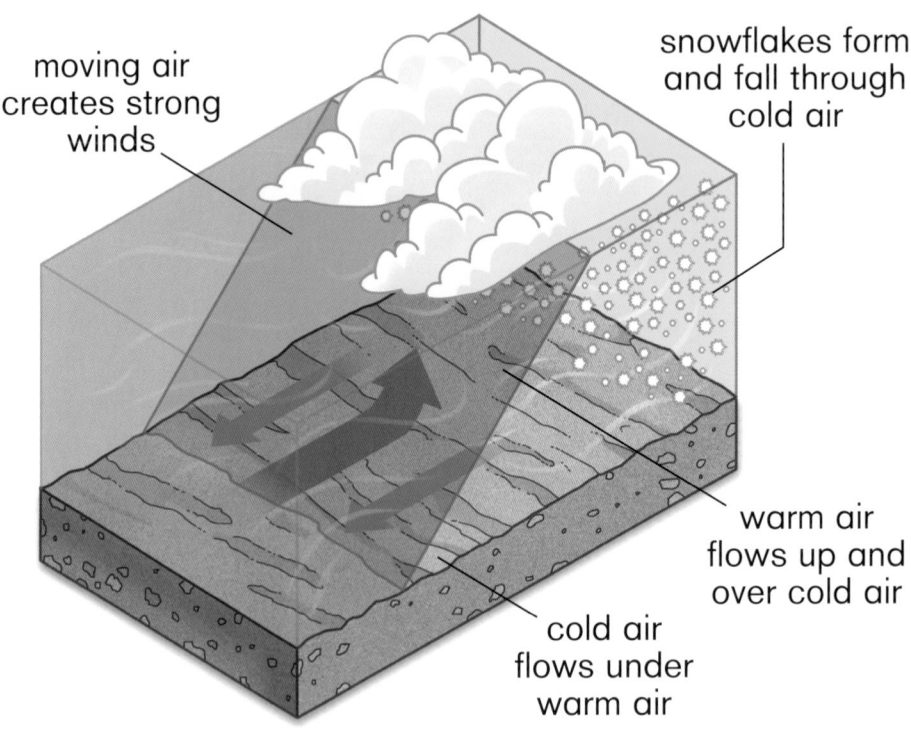

moving air creates strong winds

snowflakes form and fall through cold air

warm air flows up and over cold air

cold air flows under warm air

BLIZZARD FACTS

- There are different stories about where the word *blizzard* comes from. Long ago, it was used to describe things like a hard hit or a gunshot. Then, in the 1870s, an Iowa newspaper used *blizzard* to describe a terrible snowstorm. Soon that became the major meaning of the word.

- A January 1888 blizzard became famous as the Schoolchildren's Blizzard. Lots of children were sent home early from school because of the storm. But that was a long time before there were school buses. Many children got lost in the storm and died on their way home.

- Windchill measures how cold it is when the wind blows. Let's say the temperature falls to 5°F (−15°C) and blizzard winds are 35 miles (56 km) per hour. The windchill then equals −21°F (−29°C). Uncovered skin can freeze in just a minute.

- Wearing a hat is very important when it is cold. People lose lots of heat through their heads.

- Even Hawaii sometimes has blizzards in its highest mountains!

Further Reading

Books

Chambers, Catherine. *Blizzard*. Chicago: Heinemann Library, 2007.

Figley, Marty Rhodes. *The Schoolchildren's Blizzard*. Minneapolis: Millbrook Press, 2004.

Thomas, Rick. *Whiteout! A Book about Blizzards*. Minneapolis: Picture Window Books, 2005.

Websites

Federal Emergency Management Agency–FEMA for Kids
http://www.fema.gov/kids/wntstrm.htm
On this site, you can read "The Disaster Twins" blizzard story, play the snowman game, or become a Disaster Action Kid.

Weather Wiz Kids
http://www.weatherwizkids.com/winter_storms.htm
A TV meteorologist created this website. Visit to learn more about winter storms. On this site, you can figure out windchill and do other experiments.

Web Weather for Kids
http://eo.ucar.edu/webweather/blizzardhome.html
Find science activities and games on this website. You can also learn more about winter weather and read about blizzard safety.

Glossary

blizzard: a snowstorm with strong winds. Blizzard winds blow around 35 miles (56 km) per hour or more for at least three hours. The winds blow snow that makes it hard to see more than 0.25 miles (0.4 km).

frostbite: harm caused when a body part freezes. Frostbite often hurts a person's fingers or toes first.

meteorologist: a scientist who studies the weather

snowmobile: a machine that people can ride over snow

temperature: a measure of how hot or cold it is. Temperature can be measured in degrees Fahrenheit (°F) or Celsius (°C).

tornadoes: dangerous, spinning windstorms

windchill: a measure of how cold the wind makes the air temperature feel

Index